Cranbury
Public
Library

23 North Main St. • Cranbury, NJ 08512
(609) 655-0555

D1518064

WE CAN READ about NATURE!™

IT'S THE WIND

by Catherine Nichols

BENCHMARK BOOKS

MARSHALL CAVENDISH
NEW YORK

With thanks to
Susan Jefferson, first grade teacher at Miamitown
Elementary, Ohio, for sharing her innovative teaching
techniques in the Fun with Phonics section.

Benchmark Books
Marshall Cavendish Corporation
99 White Plains Road
Tarrytown, New York 10591
Website: www.marshallcavendish.com

Text copyright © 2002 by Marshall Cavendish

All rights reserved. No part of this book may be reproduced in any form
without written permission from the publisher.

Photo Research by Candlepants, Inc.

Cover Photo: Corbis/Jay Syverson

The photographs in this book are used by permission and through the courtesy of:
Corbis: Dave Bartruff, 4; Philip James Corwin, 5; Tony Azzura, 6; Julie Habel, 7; Joe
McDonald, 8; Ron Watts, 9 (top); Joel W. Rogers, 9 (bottom); James A. Sugar, 10;
Richard Cummins, 11; Karen Huntt Mason, 12-13; The Purcell Team, 15, 24; Layne
Kennedy, 16; Annie Griffiths Belt, 17; Jim Zuckerman, 18; H. David Seawell, 19; Paul
Almasy, 20; Kevin Flemming, 21; Japack Company, 22; David Muench, 23; Bill Ross, 25;
Neil Rabinowitz, 26; Jan Butchofsky-Houser, 27. *The Image Bank:* Terje Rakke, 28-29.

Library of Congress Cataloging-in-Publication Data

Nichols, Catherine.
It's the wind / by Catherine Nichols
p. cm. — (We can read about nature)
Includes index (p.32).
ISBN 0-7614-1254-9
1. Winds—Juvenile literature. [1. Winds.] I. Title. II. Series.

QC931.4 .N53   2001   551.51'8—dc21   2001025041

Printed in Italy

1 3 5 6 4 2

Look for us inside this book.

flag

hurricane

kite

pinwheel

rock

sail

sand dunes

storm

tornado

weather vane

windmill

windsurfer

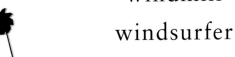

What is making this pinwheel spin and this flag flap?

Did you guess?
It's the wind.

Wind is air that moves.
Some winds blow gently.

Some winds blow strong.

These rocks were shaped by the wind.

So were these sand dunes
and this tree.

East? West? North? South?
Which way does the wind blow?
Weather vanes let you know.

Sometimes it rains,
and the wind blows hard.
A storm is coming.
It's time to go indoors
where it's safe and warm.

A hurricane is a storm with powerful winds.

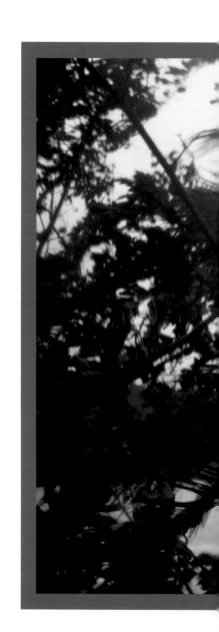

Hurricanes can bend and
break trees.

Sometimes houses are destroyed.

When a hurricane is over,
there's a lot of cleaning up to do.

A tornado is a storm
made up of whirling winds.
It sucks up everything in its path.

These horses are running away
from a tornado.

Not all winds are harmful.
Wind can be useful, too.
Windmills are machines
that run on wind.
Windmills once made flour.

Today, windmills make electricity
for people to use.

The wind helps plants to multiply.
It carries these seeds far away.

Now new plants can grow.

Look at how this bird
spreads its wings.
It's using the wind to fly.
So is this windsurfer.

Whoosh!
The wind puffs out the sails
of these boats.

It sends this balloon on a trip
across the sky.

And try flying a kite without wind!

fun with phonics

How do we become fluent readers? We interpret, or decode, the written word. Knowledge of phonics—the rules and patterns for pronouncing letters—is essential. When we come upon a word we cannot figure out by any other strategy, we need to sound out that word.

Here are some very effective tools to help early readers along their way. Use the "add-on" technique to sound out unknown words. Simply add one sound at a time, always pronouncing previous sounds. For instance, to sound out the word **cat**, first say **c**, then **c-a**, then **c-a-t**, and finally the entire word **cat**. Reading "chunks" of letters is another important skill. These are patterns of two or more letters that make one sound.

Words from this book appear below. The markings are clues to help children master phonics rules and patterns. All consonant sounds are circled. Single vowels are either long –, short ˇ, or silent ∕. Have fun with phonics, and a fluent reader will emerge.

Bossy "ar" says the letter name R.

h a R d   f a R   h a R m f u l

Bossy "or" says the word or.

s t o r m   i n d ∅ o r s   t o r n a d o   h o r s ǫ s

N o r t h

Bossy "er," "ir," and "ur" say "rrr" as if an animal is growling.

30

w e͏ͤa t h e r
rrr

s u r f e r
rrr   rrr

w h i r l i n g
rrr

p o w e r f u l
☹   rrr

h u r r i c̆ a̅ n e̸
rrr

b i r d
rrr

o̅ v e r
rrr

a̅ i r
rrr

ĕ v e r y̸ t h i̅ n g
rrr

The "ing" letter combination will always say "ing,"
whether it is part of a word or a suffix.

w i n g s

u̅ s i n g

m a̅ k i n g

c l e̸ a̸ n i n g

w h i r l i n g
rrr

r ŭ n n i n g

f l y̅ i n g

ĕ v e r y̸ t h i n g
rrr

fun facts

- A chinook is a mountain wind that is so warm it can
  melt snow.
- A storm becomes a hurricane when its wind speed
  reaches 74 miles per hour.
- A hurricane's center is called its eye. Inside the eye the
  air is calm.
- A tornado once lifted a train off its tracks and dropped
  it 80 feet away.
- A tornado that forms over water is called a waterspout.

glossary/index

about the author

Catherine Nichols has written nonfiction for young readers for fifteen years. She currently works as an editor for a small publishing company. She has also taught high-school English. Ms. Nichols lives in Jersey City, New Jersey, with her husband, daughter, and their pet Moonlight, a white cat with a long black tail.

32

CRANBURY PUBLIC LIBRARY

3 9380 00047952 8

CRANBURY PUBLIC LIBRARY
23 North Main Street
Cranbury, NJ 08512